BIBLE PROPHECY

SIGNS OF THE TIMES

LARRY HUCH

BIBLE PROPHECY

SIGNS OF THE TIMES

DEDICATION

To all of those that continue to stand with Tiz and me in support of Israel and the Jewish people.

To Anna, Brandin, Luke, Jen and Katie and my grandchildren, Asher, Judah, Aviva Shalom and Lion.

May we all "look up" with great expectancy of Jesus, our Messiah's return and remain faithful to occupy and build the Kingdom of God.

TABLE OF CONTENTS

INTRODUCTION
EYES TO SEE THE SIGNS OF GOD

The reason I wrote this book is because God wants you to have eyes to see what He is saying to you and shouting to the world around you. By having eyes to see what God is showing you, in signs and wonders, you will be able to hear His voice. You will hear His voice in the signs of the heavens – the stars, moon and sun. You will hear His voice as ancient prophecies come alive and are fulfilled. You will hear His voice and understand the meaning of numbers, letters and the appointed times or moedims which are the Feasts of the Lord. More importantly, you will hear His voice speaking to you about your future. But first, you must have eyes to see.

Let's look at some scriptures together, starting with Matthew 13:3. Great multitudes had come to hear Jesus teach. When He had finished teaching, the disciples came to Him and asked, "Why do you speak to them in parables?" The parable He had been sharing was one that is familiar to most of us. It was the portion of scripture about the sower sowing the seed.

> "³Then He spoke many things to them in parables, saying: "Behold, a sower went out to sow. ⁴ and as he sowed, some *seed* fell by the wayside; and the birds came and devoured them. ⁵ Some fell on stony places, where they did not have much earth; and they immediately sprang up because they had no depth of earth. ⁶ But when the sun was up they were

scorched, and because they had no root they withered away. [7] And some fell among thorns, and the thorns sprang up and choked them. [8] But others fell on good ground and yielded a crop: some a hundredfold, some sixty, some thirty. [9] He who has ears to hear, let him hear!" (Matthew 13:3-8)

The "seed" is God's Word. Some seeds fall by the wayside and the birds come and devour them. Others fall on stony ground and even some are surrounded by thorns, get choked out and can't survive. But in each case, God's Word and revelation is wasted, becomes unproductive, or is lost.

The Mysteries of the Kingdom

When the disciples asked Him why He spoke in parables, Jesus responded with something that is very exciting for you and me. "Because it has been given to you to know the mysteries of the Kingdom of Heaven." Jesus said to them, "It has been given to you to know."

"[10] And the disciples came and said to Him, "Why do you speak to them in parables?" [11] He answered and said to them, "Because it has been given to you to know the mysteries of the kingdom of heaven, but to them it has not been given. [12] For whoever has, to him more will be given, and he will have abundance; but whoever does not have, even what he has will be taken away from him. [13] Therefore I speak to them in parables, because seeing they do not see, and hearing they do not hear, nor do they understand." (Matthew 13:10-13)

The word know is critical to our understanding of what Jesus is saying. In John 8:32 Jesus declares, "And you shall know the truth, and the truth shall make you free." The translation doesn't communicate the deeper meaning. What Jesus was saying was this - the truth you know, receive and own, will set you free. That word know in this passage is the same one Jesus used in Matthew 13:11 when He was talking about knowing the "mysteries of the Kingdom of Heaven." You can know, receive, own and stand upon the "mysteries" He wants to reveal to you.

When Tiz and I were pastoring in Australia we had a parrot. We taught him to say, "Pay your tithes. Pay your tithes." Whenever someone would come close to his cage, he would respond, "Pay your tithes. Pay your tithes." He could "parrot" back what we taught him, but he didn't know the truth of what he was saying.

With that in mind, look again at the passage in Matthew 13, verses 13-17 where Jesus continued to answer the disciples' question, quoting from Isaiah the prophet.

"13 Therefore I speak to them in parables, because seeing they do not see, and hearing they do not hear, nor do they understand. 14 And in them the prophecy of Isaiah is fulfilled, which says: Hearing you will hear and shall not understand, And seeing you will see and not perceive; 15 For the hearts of this people have grown dull. Their ears are hard of hearing, And their eyes they have closed, Lest they should see with their eyes and hear with their ears, Lest they should understand with their hearts and turn, So that I should heal them.' 16 But blessed are your eyes for they see, and your ears for they hear; [17] for assuredly, I say to you that many prophets and righteous *men* desired to see what you see, and did not see *it,* and to hear what you hear, and did not hear *it.* (Matthew 13:13-17)

Eyes to Really See

Look at verse 16 for a moment. It says "But blessed are your eyes for they see." The word "see" here is different from what appears to be the same word "see" in verses 13 – 15. In verse 16, the word "see" has, what in the Hebrew language is called, a yod. If you were looking at it in the original text, it would appear like a comma above a letter. That small difference is critical to our understanding of this passage of scripture. The yod means the presence of God. Knowing that, go back with me to verse 13.

Matthew records the words of Jesus as "...seeing they do not see, and hearing they do not hear, nor do they understand." Because the yod is missing from the word "seeing" they had physical eyes to see, but they were unable to comprehend or understand what God was doing. But in verse 16, those that had "eyes to see" were able to receive spiritual revelation and "see" the signs from God.

This will become even clearer when we look at Exodus chapter 3 verses 1-3. Moses sees a bush that is burning.

"[1] Now Moses was tending the flock of Jethro his father-in-law, the priest of Midian. And he led the flock to the back of the desert, and came to Horeb, the mountain of God. [2] And the Angel of the LORD appeared to him in a flame of fire from the midst of a bush. So he looked, and behold, the bush was burning with fire, but the bush *was* not consumed. ³ Then Moses said, "I will now turn aside and see this great sight, why the bush does not burn." (Exodus 3:1-3)

It wasn't a spiritual vision. He actually saw the burning bush with his physical eyes. In verse 3 something interesting happens. It says, "Then Moses said "I will now turn aside and see this great sight, why the bush does not burn." What did he mean "turn aside and see?" The yod has been added here to the word "see" just as it was added to Matthew 13:16. The scripture says in Exodus 3:4-6 that Moses turned and looked with his spiritual eyes to see what God was doing.

"⁴ So when the LORD saw that he turned aside to look, God called to him from the midst of the bush and said, "Moses, Moses!" And he said, "Here I am." ⁵ Then He said, "Do not draw near this place. Take your sandals off your feet, for the place where you stand *is* holy ground." ⁶ Moreover He said, "I *am* the God of your father—the God of Abraham, the God of Isaac, and the God of Jacob." And Moses hid his face, for he was afraid to look upon God." (Exodus 3:4-6)

No Coincidences

Moses' encounter with God at the burning bush was not a coincidence. I teach all the time that in ancient Hebrew there is no word for coincidence. Not even close. "A coincidence is a remarkable concurrence of events or circumstances without apparent causal connection, accident, chance, serendipity, fortune, happenstance, providence, or a fluke."

Nothing God does is a coincidence. As you go through this book, you will see God's plan and purpose through signs in the heavens, blood moons, solar eclipses, the constellation of Virgo, the 70th anniversary of the nation of Israel and many more events that line up with Bible prophecy. These aren't coincidences. They aren't flukes. They are signs God is giving us. Each sign in its own way is a powerful revelation. Together, these signs cannot be ignored.

Don't Miss A Thing

I don't want you to miss a thing God is doing. I want you to see it all and hear His voice. You are reading this right now because you want to know what He is doing. But you might be thinking "I do want to hear God's voice, but how?" There are many ways to hear Him – as you pray, read His Word and listen to a teaching.

There is no limit to the ways God wants to speak to you and me. He wants to lead us, guide us and show us things to come. Sometimes He speaks to us in that "still, small voice" while other times He shouts to us.

It's Time to Look Up

This is a prophetic time. The Book of Luke, chapter 21, verse 28 tells us to "Look up and lift up your heads, because your redemption draws near." This is an exciting time. The signs in the sun, moon, and stars, as well as the events happening around the world are indications that we are in the end of days.

One thing I know for certain, God has a message for us right now. He wants us to share it with the whole world. Some will see, others will not. Some will hear, others will not. He wants us to see and hear what He is doing.

Tiz and I pray that God will open your eyes so that you will see and open your ears so you will hear. I pray as well that God will use you to pass on to others what He is doing so that they will see as well. We need to get ready. The Messiah is coming very soon!

CHAPTER 1

MOEDIMS - GOD'S APPOINTED TIMES

In the Book of Job, God asks a question, "Is there not an appointed time?" In Hebrew the word is moedim. It's an important word for us to understand and I will be sharing more about it with you in a moment. I think we forget that Jesus was speaking to the Jewish people in His Word. I can almost hear the inflection in His voice when He asked Job that question. It was as if He was saying, "Job, you know about this. You know about My moedims - appointed times." Many of us, maybe even you, don't have that same understanding.

What is a moedim? When are God's appointed times? Look with me at Leviticus 23:1-4 and you'll discover more about these seasons on His calendar and the Feasts of the Lord.

> "¹ And the LORD spoke to Moses, saying, ²"Speak to the children of Israel, and say to them: 'The feasts of the LORD, which you shall proclaim *to be* holy convocations, these *are* My feasts. ³ 'Six days shall work be done, but the seventh day *is* a Sabbath of solemn rest, a holy convocation. You shall do no work *on it;* it *is* the Sabbath of the LORD in all your dwellings. ⁴'These *are* the feasts of the LORD, holy convocations which you shall proclaim at their appointed times." (Leviticus 23:1-4)

God makes it clear what His feasts are and how they should be celebrated. From verse 5 of chapter 23 all the way through verse 44 and the end of the chapter, He outlines these appointed times. The Feasts of the Lord begins in the spring at Passover, around the time we celebrate the resurrection of Jesus. The second comes 50 days later and is Shavuot, or what the Church calls Pentecost. The last happens in the fall of the year and is Sukkot or the Feast of Tabernacles.

These are moedims, set aside by God each year. He releases blessings, breakthroughs, victories and miracles that you don't want to miss. Unfortunately, many do because they don't have eyes to see and ears to hear.

You Have an Appointment with God

God has made an appointment with you and me three times a year. He has told us when it is, what He wants us to do, what He will do and also how we can receive everything He has for us. But there's much more. I have a great revelation to share with you! It's found in Isaiah 55:6. Look at it with me.

"⁶Seek the LORD while He may be found, Call upon Him while He is near." (Isaiah 55:6)

During these appointed times God's presence, power, blessings and miracles are stronger than other times throughout the year. Here in the Dallas-Fort Worth Metroplex the sun shines almost all the time. There are times when it's dark, gloomy and below freezing. But those don't last long. In the summer the temperature will be above 100 degrees. So what's the difference? Intensity.

The sun shines brighter and with more intensity in the summer than in the spring, fall and winter. What does that have to do with God's appointed times? God is God 24/7. But during His moedims the "Son" is closer than at any other time.

During these times we come to the Lord. Deuteronomy 16:16 says:

> "16 Three times a year all your males shall appear before the LORD your God in the place which He chooses: at the Feast of Unleavened Bread, at the Feast of Weeks, and at the Feast of Tabernacles; and they shall not appear before the LORD empty-handed. (Deuteronomy 16:16)

We are to come to the Lord and present our First Fruits offering and we should not come empty handed. Why is that? God wants to bless us. Malachi 3:10 says:

> "10 Bring all the tithes into the storehouse, that there may be food in My house, And try Me now in this," Says the LORD of hosts, "If I will not open for you the windows of heaven and pour out for you *such* blessing that *there will* not *be room* enough *to receive it.*" (Malachi 3:10)

As you come with your First Fruits offering, God wants to open the windows of heaven over you and your family and pour out a blessing that cannot be contained. You don't want to miss this unlimited flow of God's prosperity, the end time transfer of wealth and the 7 "fat" years that are coming to those that have eyes to see and ears to hear.

CHAPTER 2

SIGNS, SEASONS, DAYS AND YEARS

If we want to see what God is doing in the end of days, we have to understand what He did in the beginning of days. In Genesis, Chapter 1, verse 14, God said, "Let there be lights in the heavens, in the firmament of the heaven, to divide day from night, and let them be for signs and seasons and appointed times for days and for years."

God tells us that He put the sun, the moon and the stars in the heavens not only to divide the day from the night, but for signs and seasons and for days and years. That's amazing. God is saying to us, "look up" and have eyes to see what I am speaking to you through these signs in the heavens. Remember, I'm not telling you these things. God is telling you! It's in His Word.

David declares in Psalm 19:1,

> "¹The heavens declare the glory of God; and the firmament shows His handiwork." (Psalm 19:1)

David said "The heavens declare the glory of God." He understood the signs in the sun, moon and stars because he knew the meaning of Genesis 1:14. God had placed them there for "signs and seasons, and for days and years." They were not there by accident. David goes on to write in Psalm 8:3-5:

> "³When I consider Your heavens, the work of Your fingers, the moon and the stars, which You have ordained, ⁴What is

man that You are mindful of him, And the son of man that You visit him? [5] For You have made him a little lower than the angels, And You have crowned him with glory and honor. (Psalm 8:3-5)

If David recognized the heavens, the work of God's fingers, the moon and the stars which He ordained, shouldn't you and I? They were not placed there by accident. They were not there by coincidence. God put them there for His purposes and for us to see and understand. David says in Psalms 147:4 says "He counts the number of the stars; He calls them all by name."

I find it interesting, even amazing, that all civilizations look to the stars for one reason or another. The ancient cultures of Greece, Rome, Egypt, Persia, Assyria and Babylonia interpreted the stars according to the study of astrology, not astronomy. They studied the constellations of the zodiac and made gods of what they saw in the twelve symbols. But they overlooked God who had placed the planets, stars and constellations into their heavenly formations.

God clearly has given us signs in the heavens. When God is questioning Job in Job 38:31-32 He asks, "Can you bind the cluster of the Pleiades, or loose the belt of Orion? Can you bring out Mazza Roth in its season? Or can you guide the Great Bear with its cubs?" Job is one of the oldest books of the Bible. This scripture makes it clear that the zodiac and the constellations were already known and revealed. God Himself called them "the hosts of heaven."

For centuries, men navigated the open seas using geometry, astronomy and special instruments to guide them in their journeys around the world. Compasses were widely used. When GPS replaced older navigational systems in 1973, calculations became much easier. But, the stars, God's signs in the heavens, still work today and always will.

If you are lost in the mountains without a compass, the North Star serves as a constant point of navigation. When the GPS of an ocean-going vessel goes out, the captain will still use the Southern Cross or the Little Dipper to get back on course. Psalm 33:4 says "For the word of the LORD is right, and all His work *is done* in truth." When God tells us something, we can trust that not only is it true today, but it will be true forever.

You may be wondering why I am sharing this with you. It's because for thousands of years people have been looking to the heavens for direction. They have journeyed across the seas, through the mountains and in the air using the stars. The sun, moon and stars have guided them in their earthly travels. My prayer, and Tiz's as well, is that God's signs in the heavens will guide you on your spiritual journey. He is always faithful.

"37It shall be established forever like the moon, Even *like* the faithful witness in the sky." Selah, Selah, Forever." (Psalm 89:37)

CHAPTER 3
ASTRONOMY AND GOD'S SIGNS

I believe there is a critical difference between the astrologer's occult interpretation of the zodiac and the intention of God to speak to us through heavenly signs and wonders.

Look with me at Isaiah 47:13.

"¹³You are wearied in the multitude of your counsels; Let now the astrologers, the stargazers and the monthly prognosticators stand up and save you from what shall come upon you."

Astrology, horoscopes and the occult aren't signs from God. There is no question about that. The Bible is making it abundantly clear that stargazers and astrologers are in danger. They are not alone. Those that seek their advice are in jeopardy as well. There is no question that God's Word condemns these practices.

Astronomy, the study of the stars, is a real science based on observation and research. Astronomers look to the heavens for understanding of the moon and the planets – everything outside the earth's atmosphere. Astronomy is one of the oldest sciences in world history.

When I take a group to Israel, I include several side trips, including one to Sepphoris or Zippori, the city where Joseph and his father sold their goods in the marketplace. At archeological sites, where ancient synagogues have been excavated, you can clearly see the signs of the zodiac on the floor, preserved for thousands of years. The question is, "Why would they put signs of the sun, moon and stars in their places of worship? The answer is clear – because God put them in the heavens for "signs and seasons."

Many Christians say, "That's not something I believe in. It's witchcraft. Astrology is of the devil. I don't believe God speaks to us through the stars and signs in the heavens!" My answer to those people is, "Yes He does." Many of you reading this book right now, agree. God speaks to me and you through signs in the heavens. He has a message in the sun, moon and stars He wants you and me to understand.

Everything God does, Satan tries to counterfeit. He twists the truth and distorts the original meaning behind God's creative meaning. Remember though, counterfeiters only copy what is real.

The symbols of zodiac were given by God as signs in the heavens to reveal what is to come. Let me share a few examples with you. The constellation of Leo – Jesus is the representation of a lion. He is the Lion of the Tribe of Judah. The constellation of Orion – Jesus is shown as lifted up and crushes the head of the serpent just as the scripture declares in Genesis 3:15. "And I will put enmity between you and the woman, and between your seed and her Seed; He shall bruise your head, and you shall bruise His heel."

What did the wise men of the east see in the heavens that announced the coming of Jesus? They saw the stars and the constellations.

When you decorate your Christmas tree, place the star at the top to commemorate and celebrate the birth of Jesus, remember that it was the Star of Bethlehem that guided the wise men from the east. They followed the sign in the heavens to the birthplace of the Messiah. The wise men had eyes to see and ears to hear. Matthew 2:12 says "Then, being divinely warned in a dream that they should not return to Herod, they departed for their own country another way."

Jesus talked about signs in the heavens. He said that there would be signs in the moon, in the sun and among the stars in Luke 21:25. Then in verse 28, He tells us to "Look up and lift up your heads!" Why? Because "Our redemption draws nigh."

When Jesus said, "Look up," He is talking about physically looking up – fixing your eyes on the heavens, looking for signs in the skies. In His great love and compassion for us, the Lord didn't want us to miss out on what would happen through the centuries of prophecy. What Jesus was saying is as these various signs of the end times begin to happen, get ready, because something powerful is about to occur.

But then Jesus repeats Himself. "Lift up your heads" He reveals the spiritual response to these signs. When you see these things begin to happen, don't be discouraged or downcast. Lift your heads in faith and with confidence because you have a living hope and strong expectation of your coming redemption.

CHAPTER 4

BLOOD MOONS AND SOLAR ECLIPSES

Science is confirming the Bible in ways we've never seen before. Even the world's most renowned astronomers and those that work for NASA, have been writing about blood moons and solar eclipses for years. Not only have they recorded heavenly phenomena going back throughout history, but they're constantly scanning space to predict when they will occur again.

Remarkably, every time we have had a tetrad, or sequence of four blood moons, the world has changed drastically. Many of you have already read my book "4 Blood Moons – Your Future Begins Now." In that book, I chronicled what the Lord showed me would happen between 2014 and 2015.

(The Four Blood Moons of 2014 through 2015)

At that time, seven tetrads of four blood moons, had been studied and recorded, since the time of Jesus. We were about to experience the eighth. I called it the sign of a new beginning. Let me share some of the things God showed me as I was writing the book. The importance of what happened years ago, only underscores the times we are living in now. I believe the next series of signs in the heavens will signal the start of a new season of God's appointed times and the fulfillment of end time prophecy.

The blood moons of 2014 and 2015 occurred in the following sequence. The first blood moon was on Passover 2014, the second on Sukkot (The Feast of Tabernacles) 2014, the third on Passover of 2015 and the fourth on Jubilee, the Feast of Tabernacles 2015.

With each sequence of blood moons, world events unfolded in a remarkable way. Let me share a few.

1. 162-163 AD: There was a great famine and plague. Persecution of Christians increased in the Roman Empire under the rule of Marcus Aurelius.

2. 795-796 AD: Charlemagne's successful campaigns ended centuries of Arab invasions into Western Europe.

3. 842-843 AD: The Christian Byzantine Empire defeated Islamic armies in Turkey, stopping the invasion of Eastern Europe.

4. 1493-1494 AD: The Spanish Inquisition saw the torture and expulsion of Jews from Spain. At the same time, Christopher Columbus launched his expedition to the

New World.

5. 1949-1950 AD: Israel was reborn as a nation. The Arab Israeli War was fought. The 1949 Armistice Agreement was signed.

6. 1967-1968 AD: Israel won the Six Day War and occupied the city of Jerusalem for the first time since 70 AD.

What amazing world-changing events! I want to highlight a few of these again because of their importance. You've heard the saying, "In 1492 Columbus sailed the ocean blue." In America, we all grew up hearing the importance of that date to our history, because Columbus discovered America. Let's not forget the other side of the story. King Ferdinand and Queen Isabella who ruled Spain conspired with Pope Sixtus IV to launch the brutal Spanish Inquisition. Under the guise of maintaining the Catholic form of faith, what followed was intense persecution of any who didn't convert to Catholicism, especially the Jews.

In 1492, amid anti-Semitism, Ferdinand and Isabella issued a decree to banish all Jewish people from Spain. Here is what Christopher Columbus wrote in his diary "In the same month in which their Majesties issues the edict that all Jews should be driven out of the kingdom and its territories, in the same month they gave me the order to undertake with sufficient men my expedition of discovery to the Indies."

As the Jews were being thrown out of Spain, Columbus sailed to America to find a new homeland for the Jews. It happened during the blood moon sequence of 1492 – 1494 AD.

In 1948 Israel became a nation and the world changed forever. It wasn't a coincidence. Some twenty-five hundred years before the four blood moons of 1949-1950. God said this through the prophet Ezekiel, "For I will take from among the nations, gather you out of all countries, and bring you into you own land...Then you shall dwell in the land that I gave to your fathers; you shall be My people, and I will be your God." (Ezekiel 36:24, 28).

The blood moon tetrad of 1949-1950 signaled the fulfillment of this Scripture and many others. Talk about signs, wonders and miracles! In May 1948, the United Nations officially gave the Jewish people their ancestral homeland and the State of Israel was legally established. In 1967 the city of Jerusalem came back into the hands of the Jewish people. These were signs of the time. As Jerusalem was retaken, a prophecy was fulfilled.

Signs in the heavens continue. Wars and rumors of wars fill our airwaves. Earthquakes, fires and massive storms continue. Prophecy is being fulfilled every day and seen by millions on the evening news. But many remain skeptical saying, "These things have always happened." My response to them would be, "Not to the degree we are seeing them happen right now."

We are living in a time when we need to be paying attention to what is occurring around us. We need to see things the way God sees them. We need to listen to His voice as we read His Word. As events happen around us, prophecy after prophecy is coming to pass. Nations like North Korea, Iran, Russia and

Syria are declaring, "We will wipe Israel off the map." They are bracing for nuclear war. These are all indicators of where we are on God's end time schedule. They are birth pangs. They are the beginning of many things to come. It isn't about doom and gloom because the Bible says, "When you see these things happening, look up, for your redemption is on its way."

One of the things the Bible talks about during the end of days is the great falling away. I Timothy 4:1 talks about a great apostasy.

> "[1] Now the Spirit expressly says that in latter times some will depart from the faith, giving heed to deceiving spirits and doctrines of demons." (I Timothy 4:1)

It's already happening. Fewer people are going to church. Less believe in the Bible. Recent statistics reveal that 85 percent don't even believe what God says in His Word. We need to wake up. We need to correctly discern the times. Our redemption is on the way.

CHAPTER 5

INTERPRETING PROPHECY - CAUTION AND DISCERNMENT

Whenever you are dealing with prophecy you must be cautious and discerning. A lot of what is going to happen, how it will happen and when it happens is determined by what the church does. We can speed up or delay the coming of the Lord. Many might be taken by surprise by world events, but we shouldn't be.

Let me deal with another subject briefly. Even though it's slightly off the topic, it's very important. Prophetic words, just like biblical prophecy, are often misinterpreted. If someone gives you a personal word, it shouldn't differ from what God has already spoken, or is currently speaking to you. A word of "wisdom" or "knowledge" should confirm what God is already saying to you and underscore the path and purpose He has shown you. It shouldn't send you on a spiritual rabbit trail or in a radically different direction.

Now, let's get back to the interpretation of prophecy. Bible prophecy is being fulfilled every day. Recently all people could talk about was the Revelation Chapter 12 sign.

"¹Now a great sign appeared in heaven: a woman clothed with the sun, with the moon under her feet, and on her head a garland of twelve stars. ²Then being with child, she cried out in labor and in pain to give birth. ³And another sign appeared in heaven: behold, a great, fiery red dragon having seven heads and ten horns, and seven diadems on his heads. ⁴His tail drew a third of the stars of heaven and threw them to the earth. And the dragon stood before the woman who was ready to give birth, to devour her Child as soon as it was born." (Revelation 12:1-4)

Many proclaimed that it was a sign of the end of the world. Some predicted an eminent attack on Israel. When the sign appeared none of these things happened. I don't believe the years ahead are filled with doom and gloom. Instead I believe with all my heart that the best is yet to come.

The main thing, as we look at prophecy and the most recent Revelation Chapter 12 "Virgo" sign is to make sure our heart is right with God. We need to wake up, repent and return to God. Think for a moment. Let me ask you as you are reading this book, "Are you serving God?" "Are you living for Him?" "Are you helping others?" "What are you doing to make the world a better place?" "Are you helping widows and orphans?" "Are you constantly looking for a place to be a blessing?" I want you to seriously think about your answers. As believers, we want to be blessed not just for us, but to be a blessing to others.

I don't mean to press this point, but it's the most important thing I could ask you right now. "If Jesus were to come right now, would you go, or would you be left behind?" We celebrate the Fall Festivals of Elul, Rosh Hashanah, Yom Kippur and Sukkot. The whole reason for blowing the shofar for 40 days, is to wake us up and give us a chance to return to God. Our hearts need to be right with God. He is the King, enthroned in Heaven, but He needs to be on the throne of our lives.

Two Legendary Prophecies

As I am writing this book, it is the 70th anniversary of Israel – from 1948 to 2018. Leading up to that celebration, many prophecies have been fulfilled. Everybody is talking about Israel. Current events are lining up with the rabbinical prophecy of the 12th century. The fulfillment of the end time prophecy that Jews and Gentiles will become "one new man" is coming to pass just as Paul wrote in Ephesians 2:11-15.

"11Therefore remember that you, once Gentiles in the flesh—who are called Uncircumcision by what is called the Circumcision made in the flesh by hands— 12 that at that time you were without Christ, being aliens from the commonwealth of Israel and strangers from the covenants of promise, having no hope and without God in the world. 13But now in Christ Jesus you who once were far off have been brought near by the blood of Christ. For He Himself is our peace, who has made both one, and has broken down the middle wall of separation, 15 having abolished in His flesh the enmity, *that is,* the law of commandments *contained* in ordinances, so as to create in Himself one new man *from* the two, thus making peace," (Ephesians 2:11-15)

Rabbi Judah Ben Samuel was known as one of Israel's greatest rabbis. He was known as the "Light of Israel" in his homeland of Germany. A devoted man of God, in 1215, two years before his death, he delivered a series of prophecies on the future of Judaism. He foretold the rule of the Ottomans over Jerusalem for eight jubilees. A jubilee is fifty years.

December 17, during the Battle of Jerusalem, on the first day, during the Jewish feast of Chanukah, the city of Jerusalem fell to British forces led by General Allenby. It occurred after exactly 400 years and eight jubilees under Turkish occupation.

Rabbi Ben Samuel also prophesied that even though Israel had been taken, Jerusalem would be considered a "no man's land" for one more jubilee. It would be another jubilee before Jerusalem would be retaken in 1967 during the Six Day War. Rabbi Ben Samuel had seen it all. But he saw one more thing – another jubilee, a time of preparation before the Messianic era would begin.

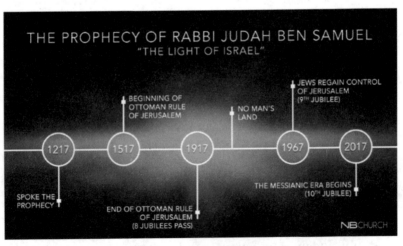

(The Prophecy of Rabbi Judah Ben Samuel)

The final part of Rabbi Ben Samuel's prophecy was echoed by another renowned teacher, Rabbi Schneerson who passed away the same month and year Tiz and I first went to Israel.

While he was alive, he made a statement I want to share with you. During his last teaching to the Orthodox community he said that the Messiah was ready to come. Schneerson added that only one more thing needed to happen before His appearing. The eyes of the Gentiles needed to be open. They had to have eyes to see and ears to hear. They would begin to understand the Jewish feasts and practice them. The celebration of Passover, Pentecost, Rosh Hashanah, Yom Kippur, and the Feast of Tabernacles would become part of their lives.

This was a powerful declaration to the Jewish community. As the prophecies of both Ben Samuel and Schneerson are fulfilled by Christians, Jews are watching as we return to the roots of our Jewish heritage.

God is using us to share the revelation, help repair the breach between Jews and Gentiles, bring down the dividing wall and stand and support the nation of Israel and the Jewish people. We aren't the only ones that are bringing this message, but we are in the forefront of the Jewish Roots movement.

I was invited by the Israeli government in 2017 to be a part of an event attended by both President Trump and Prime Minister Netanyahu. I was at the airport and was part of the delegation that welcomed President Trump to Israel. Later I attended the speeches of both leaders. As I was leaving the event, they asked me to come and have my picture taken with President Trump, First Lady Melania Trump, Prime Minister Netanyahu and his wife. There were about 10 of us waiting to be photographed.

It's a quick process. When it's your turn you step in, they take your picture, and then you exit while the next person steps in. As I was leaving, Prime Minister Netanyahu grabbed me by the arm and said, "You're Larry Huch. I watch you every day on television. God bless you for what you're teaching. God bless you for standing with Israel. Keep up the good work."

Later I had a private meeting with a member of the Israeli government and member of their Secret Service. One official said, "Pastor Larry, keep teaching what you're teaching." "I will. But why is that so important to you?" He was quick to reply to my question. "Because you are bringing us a Jesus that not only Gentiles can accept, but Jews can accept and Arabs as well. What you're teaching is the answer to the Middle East." Imagine the harvest when thousands upon thousands come into the Kingdom of God as we return to our roots and present the world with a Jewish Jesus. It's all part of the fulfillment of Bible prophecy.

CHAPTER 6

DECODING PROPHECY -
ISRAEL, THE NATIONS AND THE CHURCH

Let's decode some more prophecy. Look with me at Luke 21, starting with verse 20. Jesus says,

"²⁰But when you see Jerusalem surrounded by armies, then know that its desolation is near. ²¹ Then let those who are in Judea flee to the mountains, let those who are in the midst of her depart, and let not those who are in the country enter her. ²² For these are the days of vengeance, that all things which are written may be fulfilled. ²³ But woe to those who are pregnant and to those who are nursing babies in those days! For there will be great distress in the land and wrath upon this people. ²⁴ And they will fall by the edge of the sword, and be led away captive into all nations. And Jerusalem will be trampled by Gentiles until the times of the Gentiles are fulfilled." (Luke 21:20-24)

In this passage Jesus is prophesying about the first destruction of the temple. He is talking about Rome destroying the Temple and Jerusalem. In verse 24, He says "Jerusalem will be trampled by Gentiles." With that statement He foretells the Jews retaking the city of Jerusalem during the Six Day War of 1967. He made that prophetic declaration 2000 years ago. But His words were fulfilled in 1967 when the "times of the Gentiles" were fulfilled. A miracle happened. Even though

Israel was surrounded by all the Arab and Muslim nations, God delivered them and gave them a mighty victory. They regained Jerusalem for the first time in 2000 years.

Now, look at the next series of verses. Jerusalem is in the hands of the Jewish people again and Jesus prophesies in Luke 21 verses 25-28.

> "[25]And there will be signs in the sun, in the moon, and in the stars; and on the earth distress of nations, with perplexity, the sea and the waves roaring; [26] men's hearts failing them from fear and the expectation of those things which are coming on the earth, for the powers of the heavens will be shaken. [27] Then they will see the Son of Man coming in a cloud with power and great glory. [28] Now when these things begin to happen, look up and lift up your heads, because your redemption draws near." (Luke 21:25-28)

Before I go on, let me clarify some things. Jesus is talking about the Roman destruction of Jerusalem. That happened. Then he talks about the "Day of the Gentiles." This is where experts say the Bible is wrong. They said "Israel will never be a nation again. They are scattered all over the world. No nation has ever come back in the history of the world and become a nation again. It's never happened. It can't happen. It's impossible. They don't have a language. They don't have a people. They don't have a government. They don't have an army." God said, it's going to happen and it did in 1948 exactly the way Jesus declared it would.

Let's move on,

> "²⁹Then He spoke to them a parable: "Look at the fig tree, and all the trees. ³⁰ When they are already budding, you see and know for yourselves that summer is now near. ³¹ So you also, when you see these things happening, know that the kingdom of God is near. ³² Assuredly, I say to you, this generation will by no means pass away till all things take place. ³³ Heaven and earth will pass away, but My words will by no means pass away." (Luke 21:29-33)

Jesus is saying Jerusalem will be destroyed. It was. He said Jerusalem would be trampled under the feet of Gentiles. It was for 2000 years. But the prophecy didn't end there. God's timeline wasn't finished. There was more for us to unlock, undercover and understand.

CHAPTER 7
SOLAR ECLIPSES, CONSTELLATIONS AND SIGNS

In ancient Jewish wisdom, a lunar eclipse is a warning to the Jews, but a solar eclipse is a warning to the Gentiles. Look at Matthew 12:38-41 with me. Not everyone knows what I am going to show you.

> "³⁸Then some of the scribes and Pharisees answered, saying, "Teacher, we want to see a sign from You." ³⁹But He answered and said to them, "An evil and adulterous generation seeks after a sign, and no sign will be given to it except the sign of the prophet Jonah. ⁴⁰For as Jonah was three days and three nights in the belly of the great fish, so will the Son of Man be three days and three nights in the heart of the earth. ⁴¹The men of Nineveh will rise up in the judgment with this generation and condemn it, because they repented at the preaching of Jonah; and indeed a greater than Jonah *is* here." (Matthew 12:38-41)

Jesus answered the Pharisees and scribes and said, "An evil and adulterous generation seeks after a sign, and no sign will be given to it except the sign of the prophet Jonah." He talks to them further about Jonah. Why? Because Jonah was in the belly of the whale for three days. Jesus was in the tomb for three days before He was resurrected.

What you need to remember is that Jesus is a Jewish rabbi. He is a Jewish scholar. He is a Jewish teacher. They are saying to Him "Teacher, we want to see a sign from You." As Jews, they knew the story of Jonah and the city of Nineveh. Most Christians don't know about Jonah.

God spoke to Jonah and told him to go to Nineveh a three day journey from where he was. The city was massive and full of pagans and heathens. But God said to Jonah, I want you to go to Nineveh and preach to the people. Jonah really didn't want to go. He didn't want Nineveh to be saved and He rebelled against God. That's never a good idea, because then God had to get his attention. You don't want God getting your attention.

Jonah was swallowed by a big fish and spent three days in its belly until he spit him out, leaving him on the shores of Nineveh. Jonah preached to the people of Nineveh. He told them in 40 days God would judge them if they didn't repent.

The day that Jonah began preaching in Nineveh was the first day of the month of Elul. Right before he arrives, there was a solar eclipse called the Bear Sagel eclipse. You can look it up on the NASA's website.

The people of Nineveh saw the eclipse. When it passed a disease came upon the people of the city. They saw the eclipse as a sign from God. Jonah showed up on the first day of the month of Elul to preach and they were ready to hear. He told them you have 40 days to repent – the 30 days of Elul and 10 days of the Feast of Trumpets, which leads up to the last night and the end of Yom Kippur. All of Nineveh repented.

When Jesus is talking about the sign of Jonah, he's not limiting it to the three days. He is also talking about warnings and judgments upon the Gentiles.

On August 21, 2017, all across America, on the first day of Elul, there was a solar eclipse. Immediately following that eclipse, we experienced Hurricane Harvey, Hurricane Irma, devastation and disease. The people hit by these and other storms were good people, I'm sure. But it was a warning sign.

The last solar eclipse that brought similar levels of devastation across America was in 1918. Immediately following that eclipse there was a massive flu epidemic. Six hundred and seventy five thousand Americans died. Fifty million people worldwide died as well. Think of that! Three to five percent of the world's population at the time died in the epidemic. That same year, World War I started.

I just want to remind you again, in ancient Jewish wisdom, a lunar eclipse is a warning to the Jewish people. A solar eclipse is a warning to the Gentiles. There is still something else I want to share that is very interesting.

In 2024, seven years after this last solar eclipse there will be another solar eclipse. This time it will come right over the city of Dallas, Texas. I believe with all my heart that God is shouting to us, "Get ready. Something big is about to happen!"

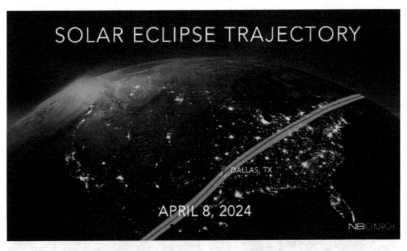

Go to Revelation, Chapter 12. Many were preparing for the end of the world. Some were packed and ready. Some were saying this is a sign of something horrible. My mom, who is 90 years old even called me. She had heard about the "Revelation 12" sign and other things that have been happening in the heavens. She asked me, "Is the rapture starting? Is something bad about to happen?" I told her "Mom when the rapture comes, it doesn't start, it is there and gone." The second thing I told her was that "I didn't believe that something bad was going to happen." I told her "I think something great is about to happen."

(The Constellation of Virgo - Modified; Original Steve Cioccolanti)

The Bible says there will be signs in the heavens. The Wise Men looked to the sky when they saw the star that announced Jesus coming 2000 years ago during Rosh Hashanah.

That same star, is the constellation that appeared again and is the constellation of Virgo, the virgin. It's the sign in the heavens referred to in Revelation 12:1-4.

"¹ Now a great sign appeared in heaven: a woman clothed with the sun, with the moon under her feet, and on her head a garland of twelve stars. ² Then being with child, she cried out in labor and in pain to give birth. ³ And another sign appeared in heaven: behold, a great, fiery red dragon having seven heads and ten horns, and seven diadems on his heads. ⁴ His tail drew a third of the stars of heaven and threw them to the earth. And the dragon stood before the woman who was ready to give birth, to devour her Child as soon as it was born." (Revelation 12:1-4)

Virgo is clothed with the sun with the moon at her feet. That configuration occurs once every year. But the constellation that was seen on September 23rd with the Virgin clothed with the sun, and the moon at her feet, also included a crown of twelve stars around her head.

I want you to get the impact of this. The exact constellations won't happen again for 7000 years. As you may already know, seven in the Hebrew understanding is the number of completion. It's the number of fulfillment. We have gone from the Hebrew year of 5777 to 5778. Eight, as you may know is the number of new beginnings.

Not only did we have the Virgin, the woman, clothed in the sun with the moon at her feet and a crown of 12 stars around her head, but the planet Jupiter passed from the womb of Virgo and was born. Waiting for that birth was another astronomical phenomenon, a swirling mass of red matter with green eyes. The Book of Revelation refers to that configuration as the "Red Dragon." It was waiting to destroy the child that has just been born. I believe that "Red Dragon" represents Satan. God saved and protected the Church from his destruction.

There are two pictures that were on the internet before September 23, 2017. The first was one released by NASA with part of the picture blocked. The second, and you can go to Google Earth and see it, is not blocked and shows the glowing red image with green eyes.

(Red Dragon – NASA, Blocked Image, You Tube, 2017)

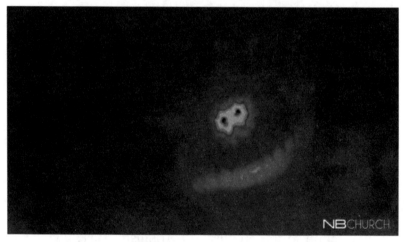

(Red Dragon – NASA, Unblocked Image, You Tube 2017)

Let me back up a little bit and share something with you that is very important. A lot of people believe that the Virgin in this passage of scripture is Israel and the baby is Jesus. I don't agree.

Let me get back to the interpretation. I believe that the Virgin is Israel, the Kingdom of God. The child is not Jesus as some have thought. When John saw this vision, Jesus had been crucified, was resurrected, and had already ascended to sit at the right hand of the throne of God. He saw the future, not the past. So, the child cannot be Jesus, the Messiah.

This sign in the heavens represents a new birth for the Church. We are coming back to our Jewish roots. When Jesus comes for the second time, He's going to find people that understand Passover. He is going to find people that have unlocked the revelation of Pentecost. He is going to see people that celebrate the Rosh Hashanah, Yom Kippur and Sukkot. As we come back to our roots and fulfill the ancient prophecies, we will provoke Jews to jealousy. They will return to their heritage and the God of Abraham, Isaac and Jacob.

Why is this so important? More books have been written by rabbis in recent years about the Jewishness of Jesus than in all the history of the Jewish people. Jews will never stop being Jews. They will continue to pray the Shema, "Hear O Israel, the Lord Thy God is one God."

Let's return to the promises of Abraham, Isaac and Jacob and the power of the first Church. I believe without a doubt that we're going to be that glorious bride, without spot and without wrinkle, living in the power of Almighty God through Jesus Christ our Lord.

With all my heart, I know we are getting ready for revival

like nothing we have seen and a moving into the fullness of God's plan and purpose.

CHAPTER 8
JOSEPH'S DREAM - 7 FAT AND 7 LEAN

There's a prophetic key I want to share with you that's connected to Joseph and Pharaoh's dream. God has been speaking to me about that dream for over a year. I kept hearing Him say, "7 fat and 7 lean."

Pharaoh, the leader of Egypt in the time of Joseph, had a dream. Pharaoh didn't understand the dream, so he went to all his wise men for an interpretation. "Tell me what this dream means." But none of them could tell him anything. I don't know about you, but I began to wonder, why couldn't Pharaoh's wise men understand? Why couldn't they interpret the dream? So Pharaoh heard about a Jew named Joseph who interpreted dreams and he sent for him.

In Genesis, Chapter 41:17-32, Joseph interprets his dream about 7 fat and 7 lean cows.

"[17] Then Pharaoh said to Joseph, "In my dream I was standing on the bank of the Nile, [18] when out of the river there came up seven cows, fat and sleek, and they grazed among the reeds. [19] After them, seven other cows came up—scrawny and very ugly and lean. I had never seen such ugly cows in all the land of Egypt. [20] The lean, ugly cows ate up the seven fat cows that came up first. [21] But even after they ate them, no one could tell that they had done so; they looked just as ugly as before. Then I woke up.

[22] "In my dream I saw seven heads of grain, full and good, growing on a single stalk. [23] After them, seven other heads sprouted—withered and thin and scorched by the east wind. [24] The thin heads of grain swallowed up the seven good heads. I told this to the magicians, but none of them could explain it to me."

[25] Then Joseph said to Pharaoh, "The dreams of Pharaoh are one and the same. God has revealed to Pharaoh what he is about to do. [26] The seven good cows are seven years, and the seven good heads of grain are seven years; it is one and the same dream. [27] The seven lean, ugly cows that came up afterward are seven years, and so are the seven worthless heads of grain scorched by the east wind: They are seven years of famine.

[28] "It is just as I said to Pharaoh: God has shown Pharaoh what he is about to do. [29] Seven years of great abundance are coming throughout the land of Egypt, [30] but seven years of famine will follow them. Then all the abundance in Egypt will be forgotten, and the famine will ravage the land. [31] The abundance in the land will not be remembered, because the famine that follows it will be so severe. [32] The reason the dream was given to Pharaoh in two forms is that the matter has been firmly decided by God, and God will do it soon." (Genesis 41:17-32)

Why was Joseph the one God used to reveal the secret? Verse 28 has the key. "This is the thing which I've spoken to Pharaoh." God is showing Pharaoh what he is about to do. "Indeed, seven years of great plenty will come upon all the land of Egypt. That seven years of famine will arise and all the plenty will be forgotten in the land of Egypt and the famine will ravage the land. So, the plenty will not be known in the land because of the famine following, for it will be very severe. And the dream was repeated to Pharaoh twice."

I want to share with you what the late Rabbi Schneerson (who in my opinion was one of the greatest Bible teachers) wrote about this important dream. "The dream experts of Egypt did indeed conceive of Joseph's interpretation of pharaoh's dream namely that 7 years of famine would follow 7 years of plenty. Yet they dismissed this interpretation from their minds because it did not account for one important detail of the dream. In Pharaoh's dream, he saw 7 lean and ugly cows that came up after the 7 fat handsome cows and stood near the fat cows upon the bend of the river. In other words, there was a time during which both sets of cows, fat and lean, coexisted simultaneously, and only after did the lean cows swallow the fat cows."

So many of us have believed the misinterpretation of the dream. But now, we can know the truth. I believe the truth about the interpretation of Pharaoh's dream is a prophetic word for us today. Ancient Jewish wisdom teaches that when something is repeated, there is a secret that needs to be revealed. The dream was repeated to Pharaoh a second time. Verse 32 declares:

"32And the dream was repeated to Pharaoh twice because the thing *is* established by God, and God will shortly bring it to pass." (Genesis 41:32)

Why is it that when Joseph interpreted the dream, Pharaoh said "That's it?" If you look at the dream the way most preachers describe it and Christians read it, it doesn't appear to be difficult to understand. There were seven fat cows. There were seven lean cows. Seven fat years followed by seven lean years. But if you read the scriptures more closely the meaning is much deeper.

The Bible says in Genesis 41:3 that Pharaoh saw seven fat cows and then he saw seven lean cows, standing side-by-side. Most have interpreted this passage as seven fat years followed by seven lean years. If you read the same passage in Hebrew, it says seven fat cows stood side-by-side with the seven lean cows.

Cows were an important symbol in ancient Egyptian culture and prophecy. Egyptians worshipped a goddess of the cow called Henthorn, the symbol of fate. Whenever a baby was going to be born, they would see a vision of seven cows and the seven cows would tell the future or the fate of the baby that was being born. Why is this important right now? Because on September 23rd, 2017, when the constellation of Virgo appeared in the heavens, the Church was reborn. These seven cows are telling us what the fate of the church is going to be.

7 Fat or 7 Lean - Which Will You Experience?

Within the Church, some of us will experience seven fat years and others the exact opposite, seven lean years. What will determine the difference? I can answer that question. It will be your service to God. In Matthew 24 and Luke 21, two are in bed and one is taken and one is left. Two are in the field and one is taken while the other is left. That's the way it will be with the seven years of fat and seven years of lean.

During Rosh Hashanah and Yom Kippur, ancient Jewish wisdom says, God opens the Book of Life to see who has served Him and brought increase to His kingdom. What prosperity and blessing you receive will be determined by how you served and not just by what you believed

The sign of Joseph is this. Some in the Church will be left behind. Some will be taken and caught up. Some will be living in the blessing of God. Others will miss the abundance God has for them. God has placed before you, life and death, blessing and cursing. He says, "Choose life." Serve God. Live for Him. Serve Him with all your heart. Help build the Kingdom. If you do that, then you will experience the fat and not the lean.

I believe there's a great revival coming. I believe there's a great outpouring of God's blessing ahead. I know everything we put our hands to will succeed and prosper because God is faithful to His promises. I have no doubt the best is yet to come. The future is not about doom and gloom. What we are seeing are birth pangs. What we are hearing is God's warning.

The Lord could come today. I really don't know when He's coming. What I do know is that those who are paying attention to His Spirit, reading His Word and living for Him will be the head and not the tail. We will be the lenders and not the borrowers. We will receive God's end time transfer of wealth and be

His bankers during these end times.

I believe God is going to give us 7 fat years. If that happens, we will be living a "good measure, pressed down and shaken together and overflowing" life. We will be in revival. Those of us who are serving God with all our hearts, will not only have enough, we will have more than enough stored up to see us through anything that comes after those seven fat years.

Now let's put the appearance of the "7000 Year Sign" with "Joseph's Sign." The seven cows that Pharaoh saw determined the fate of unborn babies. The baby that was birthed on September 23rd represents the Church. We are the salt of the earth. If you and I aren't being "salt" the Bible says we are good for nothing. We need to think about how salty we are. The Church is losing its effectiveness. It's time for us to change and God is giving us His warning.

The sign of the cows is the fate of the Church. Those who will bless Israel, God will bless. I believe we are headed for seven years of the most amazing outpouring of God's power, anointing and blessings we've ever seen. He is going to transfer the wealth of the wicked into the hands of the faithful. But you must decide. Who will you serve? What will you choose? Life or death, blessing or cursing, fat or lean? I know what I'm going to do. I know who I serve. I choose life. I bless Israel. I'm going to be one of the fat cows. I'm going to live in the blessing of God for 7 fat years.

CHAPTER 9
ISRAEL – 70 YEARS OF MIRACLES

In 2018, Israel celebrates its 70th anniversary as a nation. The number 70 is the Hebrew letter Ayin, which is the 16th letter in the alphabet and means "having eyes to see." God's Word says that blessed are those that have eyes to see. You are blessed if you see what God is trying to show us. Moses saw the burning bush and he turned aside to see what was happening. The word to see is the Hebrew word va-yaar.

When Moses saw the burning bush, he turned to see. But the Word mentions that he "saw again." How can you see something that you have already seen? When he turned to see, it is the same Hebrew word va-yaar. But this time it has a yod, a small Hebrew letter that looks like a comma, which means the presence of God. Moses saw something physical – the burning bush. But he turned to see again. He wanted to see and understand what God was doing. My prayer is that you see what God is doing right now and get ready.

In Hebrew there are levels of supernatural wisdom and understanding based upon the word P-R-D-S which means the following: the first level is P'shat, the second is Remes, the third is Drash and the last Sod. In mid-2018, Israel celebrates its 70th anniversary. Here is the secret revealed in the numerical values. 70 is the number for sod and also the numerical equivalent for the word see. Ten is the number for yod, seven the number for perfection and eight, the number of supernatural victory. But there's more I want to share with you. Abraham was born one thousand, nine hundred and forty eight years from creation. Israel became a nation in 1948. According to scholars, Abraham entered into Israel, the Promised Land at the age of 76, 2024 years since God declared "Let there be light."

A Nation Born in One Day

God has always had a plan for the Jewish people and the land of Israel. It is clear in this passage from Isaiah 66:7-8.

> "[7] Before she was in labor, she gave birth; Before her pain came, She delivered a male child. [8] Who has heard such a thing? Who has seen such things? Shall the earth be made to give birth in one day? *Or* shall a nation be born at once? For as soon as Zion was in labor, She gave birth to her children." (Isaiah 66:7-8)

The prophet Isaiah's words, breathed by God, were fulfilled in 1948 when the nation of Israel was miraculously born. I don't use the word miraculous lightly. The word miraculous means "occurring through divine or supernatural intervention." It was a miracle. Only God could have "gathered the Jewish people from the nations of the world" and made them a nation again. During Israel's 70th anniversary amazing things are going to happen. We just need to have "eyes to see."

What the Numbers Say

Biblical numerology holds the hidden meaning behind the

number 70 and gives us a glimpse into why this once in a life-time celebration is so important. If you have read my books or listened to me teach, you know something about numbers.

The number seven is seen throughout scripture. There are 7 weeks from the feast of Passover to the observance of Pentecost. There are 7 branches in the temple menorah. Jesus shed His blood 7 times for our salvation, wholeness and freedom. The High Priest sprinkled the blood of the sacrifice 7 times on the altar on the Day of Atonement. There are 7 biblical feasts. The musical scale is made up of 7 notes. There are 7 colors in the rainbow. In the Book of Revelation there are 7 churches, 7 angels, 7 seals and 7 trumpets. I could go on, but I wanted you to see why the meaning of numbers is so critical to our understanding. God is so good. He has given us what we need to understand, see and hear in the truth of His Word.

Now that you know what the number seven means, let's look at the number 10. The obvious place to start is in the Torah and the 10 Commandments in Exodus 20. Let's go a little deeper using Leviticus 27:30.

> "30 And all the tithe of the land, *whether* of the seed of the land *or* of the fruit of the tree, *is* the LORD's. It *is* holy to the LORD, a tithe, a tenth of everything from the land, whatever grain from the soil or fruit from the trees, belongs to the Lord. It is holy to the Lord." (Leviticus 27:30)

This isn't a book on tithing. But the important thing to notice is that the number 10 designates what is "holy" to God. Let me explain more using some familiar scriptures, beginning with Matthew 5:13. Jesus tells His disciples that they are "the salt of the earth." In verse 14 He says they are "the light of the world." In verses 17-18 He adds the following:

> "¹⁷Do not think that I came to destroy the Law or the Prophets. I did not come to destroy but to fulfill. ¹⁸ For assuredly, I say to you, till heaven and earth pass away, one jot or one tittle will by no means pass from the law till all is fulfilled." (Matthew 5:17-18)

In this passage of scripture, Jesus uses two words we can only understand if we look at them in the original language. Jot is the Hebrew word yod. The closest English transliteration from the Greek is "Iota." Jesus also mentioned "tittle" which is the Hebrew word "dalat." That's a study for another time. For now, let's focus on the word yod.

Yod is the tenth letter in the Hebrew alphabet. The smallest, it is actually a dot or tiny stroke of the pen, which looks like a comma. Jesus said that this part of the alphabet, the yod cannot be removed from God's Word. Why?

So many times, when we read this passage, or hear it taught, we think Jesus was saying we are not to remove the smallest of God's words. That is true, but there's more. The yod means much more. In the Hebrew language, the yod represents God Himself, His presence and power.

The number 10 is seen throughout the Old Testament. Once God created the world, there were 10 generations from Adam to Noah and another 10 from Noah to Abraham. There were 10 plagues in Egypt. 10 miracles God performed when He delivered His people. 10 attributes of God's sanctity and holiness. There are many more examples in scripture, but I will stop with these. I want to move on to the number 70.

The meaning behind the number seventy tied to Israel's anniversary from 1948 to 2018 is a combination of 7 and 10. As I mentioned earlier, in Hebrew, 70 is the numerical equivalent of the 16th letter and the word "Ayin" which means "eyes to see."

Seventy is seen throughout the scriptures. God placed 70 nations in the world. During the Feast of Sukkot (the Feast of Tabernacles) 70 oxen were sacrificed, one for each nation. Daniel's prophecy of the end of days is laid out in 70 weeks. Israel was released from Babylon after 70 years of captivity. In 70 A.D. Rome destroys Jerusalem and the Second temple. There were 70 members in the Sanhedrin.

One of the most interesting passages that mentions the number 70 is in Luke 10:1-2.

> "¹After these things the Lord appointed seventy others also, and sent them two by two before His face into every city and place where He Himself was about to go. ² Then He said to them, "The harvest truly *is* great, but the laborers *are* few; therefore pray the Lord of the harvest to send out laborers into His harvest." (Luke 10:1-2)

And Luke 10:17-18.

> "¹⁷ Then the seventy returned with joy, saying, "Lord, even

the demons are subject to us in Your name." [18] And He said to them, "I saw Satan fall like lightning from heaven." (Luke 10:17-18)

Seventy – Division or Unity?

I believe that the 70th anniversary of Israel will launch us into a season of tremendous joy and blessing where God's power is poured out on the Earth and in our lives. We will experience unprecedented supernatural signs, wonders and miracles. How can I say this with such assurance?

Notice in Luke 10:17-18 that Jesus appointed and sent 70 out with an anointing to every city He had visited during His earthly ministry and first coming. But it will happen again right before His return and second coming. Here's the key to understanding the importance of "the seventy."

The number 70 has two other meanings. It can either signify division or unity. Look with me at Genesis 11:1-9, where a series of events happened that changed all of mankind.

> "[1]Now the whole earth had one language and one speech.
> [2]And it came to pass, as they journeyed from the east, that they found a plain in the land of Shinar, and they dwelt there. [3]Then they said to one another, "Come, let us make bricks and bake *them* thoroughly." They had brick for stone, and they had asphalt for mortar. [4]And they said, "Come, let us build ourselves a city, and a tower whose top *is* in the heavens; let us make a name for ourselves, lest we be scattered abroad over the face of the whole earth." [5]But the LORD came down to see the city and the tower which the

sons of men had built. ⁶And the LORD said, "Indeed the people *are* one and they all have one language, and this is what they begin to do; now nothing that they propose to do will be withheld from them. ⁷Come, let Us go down and there confuse their language, that they may not understand one another's speech." ⁸So the LORD scattered them abroad from there over the face of all the earth, and they ceased building the city. ⁹Therefore its name is called Babel, because there the LORD confused the language of all the earth; and from there the LORD scattered them abroad over the face of all the earth." (Genesis 11:1-9)

The people built a tower to the heavens, known as the Tower of Babel, to make themselves equal with God. But God was displeased, destroyed the tower and scattered them from Babel all over the face of the earth. He divided one nation into 70, all speaking different languages. No longer could they speak "one language" but many. Babel came to mean "confusion." That is why 70 carries the meaning of both division and confusion.

The other meaning of 70 is unity. This is seen clearly in Genesis 46:27 when Jacob and his household travelled back to Egypt to be with his Joseph and his household.

"²⁷And the sons of Joseph who were born to him in Egypt *were* two persons. All the persons of the house of Jacob who went to Egypt were seventy." (Genesis 46:27)

This passage says that all the offspring of Joseph born in Egypt were two persons. Yet all the offspring of Jacob were seventy. In some translations the word soul is used to describe

Jacob's household of "70 soul." The word soul here is not a misprint. The scripture says soul not souls to reveal how many were part of Jacob's household. Why would the singular and not the plural be used? Ancient Jewish wisdom says that the unity was so great among them that God saw Jacob's household as "one soul, or one man."

As we join the Jewish people and Israel in celebrating 70 years as a nation, God is bringing unity. Paul writes about it in the Book of Ephesians, Chapter 2:14-18. He describes a time when both Jews and Gentiles are unified. He calls the miraculous union "one new man" where there is no middle wall of division between them.

"14 For He Himself is our peace, who has made both one, and has broken down the middle wall of separation, 15 having abolished in His flesh the enmity, *that is,* the law of commandments *contained* in ordinances, so as to create in Himself one new man *from* the two, *thus* making peace, 16 and that He might reconcile them both to God in one body through the cross, thereby putting to death the enmity. 17 And He came and preached peace to you who were afar off and to those who were near. 18 For through Him we both have access by one Spirit to the Father." (Ephesians 2:14-18)

God's Commanded Blessing

As Christians around the world we stand with Israel as one, Jew and Gentile together. One of my wife Tiz's favorite scriptures, Psalm 133:1-3, tells of God's blessing when people walk in unity.

"[1]Behold, how good and how pleasant *it is f*or brethren to dwell together in unity! [2] *It is* like the precious oil upon the head, Running down on the beard, The beard of Aaron, Running down on the edge of his garments.[3] *It is* like the dew of Hermon, Descending upon the mountains of Zion; For there the LORD commanded the blessing—Life forever-more." (Psalm 133:1-3)

As Jews and Gentiles come together in unity as "one new man" God promises a "commanded" blessing. He does not release His blessing He "commands" it. I believe as you and I continue to stand with, and support, the Jewish people and the land of Israel, we will receive the "commanded" blessing.

I believe these unprecedented blessings are timed perfectly to coincide with Israel's 70th anniversary. The increased teaching of the Jewish roots of the Christian faith and the building of an army of the "one new man." Those that choose to bless Israel will experience the 7 fat years of blessing that have already begun.

The 70th anniversary of Israel marks a time when God is going to give us insight, wisdom and revelation. Everything that we touch, God is going to multiply. We may not be going to Heaven yet, but are going to start living in the reality of the Kingdom of God. We're heading into the most abundant season, both spiritually and financially. We will go from glory to glory to glory.

The Prophecy of Nations

Look with me at another prophecy, out of Zechariah 14:16.

"It shall come to pass that everyone who is left of all the nations."

Think for a minute about the Church's history of replacement theology. Nearly every denomination has blamed the Jews for killing Jesus. But, the Jewish people are our family. They are our brothers and sisters. They gave us the Torah, the prophets and Jesus our Messiah. We are grafted in. Go back to verse 16 and 17 for a moment.

> "¹⁶ It shall come to pass that everyone who is left of all the nations, which came against Jerusalem, shall go up from year to year to worship the King, the Lord of hosts and keep the Feast of Tabernacles. ¹⁷And it shall be that whichever of the families of the earth do not come up to Jerusalem on them there will be no rain." (Zechariah 14:16-17)

There is a blessing for those who worship the King of Kings and Lord of Lords. There is prosperity for those that celebrate the Feast of Tabernacles. Those that return to the Jewish roots and have eyes to see and ears to hear are those who, I believe, will see the seven fat years. But those that do not have eyes to see and ears to hear will have seven lean years.

The Wise and Foolish Virgins

Jesus taught about the times in which we are living in the parable of the wise and foolish virgins found in Matthew 25:1-13. This passage of scripture reminds us to be watchful for we do not know when the bridegroom comes.

"[1] At that time the kingdom of heaven will be like ten virgins who took their lamps and went out to meet the bridegroom. [2] Five of them were foolish and five were wise. [3] The foolish ones took their lamps but did not take any oil with them. [4] The wise ones, however, took oil in jars along with their lamps. [5] The bridegroom was a long time in coming, and they all became drowsy and fell asleep. [6] "At midnight the cry rang out: 'Here's the bridegroom! Come out to meet him!' [7] "Then all the virgins woke up and trimmed their lamps. [8] The foolish ones said to the wise, 'Give us some of your oil; our lamps are going out.' [9] "'No,' they replied, 'there may not be enough for both us and you. Instead, go to those who sell oil and buy some for yourselves.' [10] "But while they were on their way to buy the oil, the bridegroom arrived. The virgins who were ready went in with him to the wedding banquet. And the door was shut. [11] "Later the others also came. 'Lord, Lord,' they said, 'open the door for us!' [12] "But he replied, 'Truly I tell you, I don't know you.' [13] "Therefore keep watch, because you do not know the day or the hour." (Matthew 25:1-13 NIV)

Notice that there are 10 virgins mentioned, the number of yod which is the presence and power of God. These virgins were born again. Their sins were forgiven. But when Jesus, the bridegroom was delayed, they slept. They let their oil run out. They were in the dark when the bridegroom arrived.

When I accepted Jesus Christ as my Lord and Savior it was a very different time. It was the late 70's. Hal Lindsey's book "The Late Great Planet Earth" on Bible prophecy was a best-seller.

The Christians I knew thought Jesus could return any minute. But now, many Christians have fallen "asleep." Churches are "visitor friendly" and don't talk much about prophecy and end time events. Stay in the light. Be watchful. Jesus, our Messiah is coming again soon.

Watchmen on the Wall - A Warning to Prepare

The Bible says the wicked servant says the master delays his coming. The Messiah could return before you turn the next page in this book. You and I need to be ready. We need to pay attention. Jesus could return any time. Prophecy is being fulfilled daily. The prophet John in the Book of Revelation recorded what he saw. He witnessed men's skin melting off of them. He saw cities disappearing in a vapor. Things flying. Nations right now are preparing for nuclear war. The prophet declared that there need to be those that will be watchful and sound a warning. But if the watchmen refuse to stand the watch and will not declare a warning to those in peril, the blood of those people will be on their hands. You and I need to be on the wall, sounding the warning. We need to be ready and help others to prepare for Jesus' return.

CHAPTER 10

REBUILDING THE TABERNACLE OF DAVID

God has declared that He will raise up the Tabernacle of David. When God told David to build Him a tabernacle He said that there should be "no middle wall" dividing Jews and Gentiles. That's in verse 12 of Amos 9.

> "¹²That they may possess the remnant of Edom, And all the Gentiles who are called by My name, "Says the Lord who does this thing." (Amos 9:12)

So, in the Tabernacle of David there was no division between Jews and Gentiles. Also, there was no veil between God and the people. He walked among the people and signs, wonders and miracles were present. The praise and worship was supernatural and prophetic.

There will be no middle wall in the rebuilt tabernacle. Paul tells us in Ephesians 2:14-15 that there will not be two – Jews and Gentiles, but "one new man." As more Christians learn the Jewish roots of their faith the wall comes down. When believers see a "fully Jewish Jesus" division melts away. As we stand and support Israel, unity is the result. As our president leads the country to stand and support our ally and friend, Israel, (the only true democracy in the Middle East) the breach between Jews and Christians will be repaired.

Behold the Days Are Coming

Look with me at Amos 9:13-15.

"13Behold, the days are coming," says the Lord, "When the plowman shall overtake the reaper, And the treader of grapes him who sows seed; The mountains shall drip with sweet wine, And all the hills shall flow with it. 14 I will bring back the captives of My people Israel; They shall build the waste cities and inhabit them; They shall plant vineyards and drink wine from them; They shall also make gardens and eat fruit from them. 15 I will plant them in their land, And no longer shall they be pulled up from the land I have given them," Says the Lord your God." (Amos 9:13-15)

An End Time Transfer of Wealth

Prosperity and salvation go hand in hand. God wants to bring us into a place of abundance and supernatural prosperity.

When the Jews were leaving Egypt, which was a place of slavery and bondage, God told Moses to tell the children of Israel this in Exodus 11:2,

"2 Speak now in the hearing of the people, and let every man ask from his neighbor and every woman from her neighbor, articles of silver and articles of gold." (Exodus 11:2)

When the children of Israel were freed from Egypt by the hand of God they also experienced the first transfer of wealth. God will pour out His Spirit in these days, on all flesh and there will be a great outpouring. I believe there will also be an end time transfer of wealth.

Amos 9:13 says "The hills shall flow with sweet wine." Wine is a sign of two things in scripture. First it is symbolic of the covenant and promises of God. Second, it is a symbol of joy. God is waiting and ready to pour out His promises and joy on those of us who are "grafted into" the rich heritage and covenant of Abraham, Isaac and Jacob.

Nehemiah 8:10 records these words.

> "10 Then he said to them, "Go your way, eat the fat, drink the sweet, and send portions to those for whom nothing is prepared; for *this* day *is* holy to our Lord. Do not sorrow, for the joy of the LORD is your strength." (Nehemiah 8:10)

As you are reading this book, I pray that God will begin to pour out His blessing in abundance and that you will be filled to overflowing with His joy. May God not only provide everything you need, but in good measure, pressed down, shaken together and over flowing. I believe that you and I both will experience more than enough so we can "send portions to those for whom nothing is prepared."

I pray also that you will have fresh revelation and "eyes to see" what God is doing now and is going to do in the days, months and years to come. Get ready, miraculous things are about to happen!

CHAPTER 11

THE GENTILES AND ALIYAH

God made a promise to return His people, the Jews, back to Israel. I want to show you a prophetic part of the scripture in Amos 9, verses 14-15.

> "¹⁴I will bring back the captives of My people Israel;
> They shall build the waste cities and inhabit them;
> They shall plant vineyards and drink wine from them;
> They shall also make gardens and eat fruit from them.
> ¹⁵I will plant them in their land, and no longer shall they be
> pulled up from the land I have given them says the Lord your
> God." (Amos 9:14-15)

God declares that He will bring back the captives to Israel. After the time of Jesus, in 70 AD Rome destroyed the second temple and drove the Jewish people from Jerusalem and parts of Israel. Titus commemorated the decisive moment with a special coin engraved with the words Judea Captiva. The names of Judea and Israel were also removed from all maps and official documents to ensure that the existence of Israel would be removed from everyone's memory. Instead the name Palestine was instituted. The people tied to the area were not even Middle Eastern, but European, which adds to today's questions surrounding Palestine and its rights to the land. The Jews return from captivity to their rightful homeland, is not a political issue with a controversial agenda, but a prophetic fulfillment of God's promise to the Jewish people.

The scriptures Ezekiel 11:17 and Isaiah 43:5-7, among others from God's Word, record His plan to bring the Jewish people back. Isaiah 49:22 shows the heart of God and His special plan for the Jewish people and their land.

> "22Thus says the Lord GOD: "Behold, I will lift My hand in an oath to the nations, And set up My standard for the peoples; They shall bring your sons in *their* arms, And your daughters shall be carried on *their* shoulders." (Isaiah 49:22)

Not only will God bring the children back to Israel from the nations, but He said that the Gentiles will help them to return to their homeland. For 2,000 years, Gentiles have often been the enemies of the Jews. They killed Jesus, destroyed Jerusalem and the temple. Russia, Portugal and Spain with their inquisition brought suffering to the Jewish people. The Holocaust murdered over six million Jews and left survivors traumatized for the rest of their lives. Anti-Semitism flourished and denominational churches widely taught replacement theology generation after generation. Still, God has chosen Gentiles to bring the Jews back to Israel from the corners of the earth. They will be part of the returning or "Aliyah" of the Jewish people.

The Hebrew word aliyah means "elevation" or "going up." In the synagogue, it is used to refer to the honor of being called up to read the Torah. In the Book of Genesis, the word was used to describe Jacob's bones being brought from Egypt to Israel. For generations, Jews of every age have been returning to Israel. Now, more than ever, men, women and children are coming back to their homeland.

CHAPTER 12
TIKKUN OLAM – REPAIRING A BROKEN WORLD

God requires each of us to do what in Hebrew is called "tikkun olam" - repair a broken world. Matthew 5:16 says:

"¹⁶Let your light so shine before men, that they may see your good works and glorify your Father in heaven." (Matthew 5:16)

Along with ministry partners and friends around the world, we have been able to provide outreaches to people across the globe. Built orphanages, support schools and provide 50,000 meals a month to hungry children. Partnered with friends in Israel at B'nai Zion Hospital, Ahava Children's Home and Netivyah Ministries. Helped build "safe rooms" for children. Feed and care for Holocaust survivors. Send gifts and supplies to IDF soldiers. Bought Mobile ICU ambulances providing emergency care on the streets of Jerusalem and surrounding areas. We have also helped Jewish families aliyah to Israel. We are continuing to do all these things as we "tikkun olam" and help repair the world around us.

This year, as we celebrate the 70ᵗʰ anniversary of Israel's nationhood, God has placed on my heart to sponsor 700 Jewish men, women and children as they make the journey back to their "promised land." You can be a part of this special outreach and bring restoration and healing to the Jewish people. Help us tear down the wall that has divided us for so long. Join the growing army that is making up the "one new man" of prophetic scripture. Because of you, and many others, the Jewish people will no longer be pulled up from the land God has promised to them.

God has given us the opportunity to participate in so many amazing projects. I want to tell you about another one. We are working with Jewish families that are planting vineyards and olive trees on land that is right outside the ancient city of Amos, now called Ma'ale Amos, where the prophet Amos lived, preached and wrote prophetic scriptures.

Grafted In Through Abraham, Isaac and Jacob

Even though we were once Gentiles and separated from God's promises and covenant we are now "grafted in." God is using us to touch the lives of Jews throughout Israel, tear down the walls that have divided us and become repairers of the breach. We are adopted into the heritage of Abraham, Isaac and Jacob.

Both Ephesians 3:6 and Romans 11:17 let us know that we have been adopted and "grafted into" the Jewish people both physically and spiritually. We are connected to the same promises that belonged to Abraham, Isaac and Jacob.

We need to be part of what God is doing right now in the earth. A friend of mine told me about a successful man who lives in Europe. During one of their conversations, he asked this man, "What is the secret to your success?" He replied quickly.

SIGNS OF THE TIMES

"Every morning I get up, go to my office and sit and look at the mountains in the distance. I pray and ask God 'What are you doing today and how can I be a part of it?" That's what you and I need to do. Look at Proverbs 3:6 with me.

> "⁶In all your ways acknowledge Him, And He shall direct your paths." (Proverbs 3:6)

Partnering With God in His Kingdom

In every area of your life, ask God what He needs you to do each day. Ask Him, "How can I partner with You and do the work of Your Kingdom?" The Hebrew word for acknowledge is yada and it means to know or to recognize. When we know and recognize what God is doing we cannot fail. Not only does God ask us to seek first His kingdom, but to seek His righteousness as well.

When most Christians hear or read the word righteousness they think of the Greek word dikaios which means to observe divine laws, be upright, faultless, innocent, or guiltless. I certainly agree that we need to live a holy, moral and righteous life as children of God. But the Hebrew word for righteousness is tzedakah and it is acts of kindness or justice.

In Matthew 6:33 when Jesus said "Seek first the kingdom of God and its righteousness." He was talking about tzedakah. He was introducing us to a great way to live. Instead of praying for God to bless us alone, God asks us to believe for more than enough to bless others.

We continue to have the privilege to be involved with projects that are changing lives around the world. Nothing brings more of God's blessings than what we do for Israel and her people.

That's why it is exciting to be a part of helping farming families at Ma'ale Amos. God is giving the land back to them. When I talked with one of the young men farming the land, I asked him "Why have you come here to this place? What brought you and your wife and children to plant in this area surrounded on all sides by Arab villages?" He was quick to answer. "I came here to the very land where a young David tended Jesse's sheep." He addressed me directly. "Pastor Larry, the very ground you are standing on, King David once stood here. You can smell God in the air. You can feel God in the wind. God is in this land forever!"

Even now as I am writing this, I can still hear his words. I pray that you will feel what I feel right now. I can't forget his words or the time I spent in the ancient village seeing prophecy fulfilled. That's why I continue to look for more ways to bless Israel.

CHAPTER 13

ONE NEW MAN

The words of the prophet Amos are being fulfilled every day in Israel. I believe God is raising you and me up to be a blessing to Israel and the Jewish people. Isaiah 58:11-12 says,

"¹¹The LORD will guide you continually, And satisfy your soul in drought, And strengthen your bones; You shall be like a watered garden, And like a spring of water, whose waters do not fail, ¹² Those from among you Shall build the old waste places; You shall raise up the foundations of many generations; And you shall be called the Repairer of the Breach, The Restorer of Streets to dwell In." (Isaiah 58:11-12)

We are anointed to break down the dividing wall between Jews and Gentiles. We are destined to be part of the "one new man" prophesied in scripture.

Not long ago I stood on the hills where King David tended his father's sheep. I helped plant olive trees and vineyards. Amos' prophetic words echoed through the hillsides. He spoke of a time when Jews and Gentiles would stand side-by-side. He foretold the rebuilding of the Tabernacle of David where there would be no middle wall of division.

One of the farmers I visited told me that he believes that someday the wine from his vineyards will be in the rebuilt Tabernacle of David. As he walks through the vineyards and tends the groves of olive trees, the words of Amos are being fulfilled.

I pray that God will touch your heart. I hope you will decide to partner with us. Help us tear down the dividing wall between Jews and Gentiles. Be a part of a growing army of "one new man." May your eyes see that now is God's appointed time.

CHAPTER 14
IN GOD WE TRUST?

I've been sharing with you about the signs God is giving us in these last days - the prophecies of Rabbi Judah Ben Samuel and Rabbi Schneerson, the four blood moons, solar eclipses and the constellation of Virgo. In earlier chapters, I showed you that Virgo, who is Israel, birthed the Church, which is Jupiter. The Red Dragon, which is Satan was waiting to destroy the Church, but God saved us.

I also revealed the meaning behind the dream of Pharaoh and Joseph's interpretation of seven fat and seven lean cows. Every one of these things are connected to Bible prophecy and the signs of the times. Jesus, the Messiah could come tomorrow. But I think we might have more time.

In the past eight years we have gone from an anti-church, anti-Israel administration that had a mosque in the White House to the exact opposite. The present administration is pro-Israel and pro-Christianity. Whether you like President Trump or you don't. Whether you are a Republican, Democrat, Independent or Libertarian isn't the issue. I believe the next seven years will be prosperous and bring blessings and the end time transfer of wealth to the people of God.

For decades we have been the frog in the pan. If you're not familiar with this expression, let me explain. If you put a frog in cool water and set it on a burner on your stovetop, it won't move. It will just sit there. The water is cool and feels like the frog's natural environment. But then, you slowly start turning up the heat. The temperature rises. The frog still doesn't move. Before long you have increased the heat and the frog is lifeless having been boiled in the pan.

I think that's exactly the way the enemy has been working in the lives of believers, in the Church and the world, particularly in America. He has slowly turned up the heat on every value we believe in until we are at boiling point and near extinction. The frog in the pan is a lot like what happened to Israel after they left Egypt.

Go to Judges 2 and look with me at this powerful scripture. Now remember, God brought Israel out of the bondage of Egypt. He warned them not to worship other gods, particularly Baal. He reminded them that He was the God who brought them out of Egypt. He gave them manna for 40 years. He struck a rock and water flowed out of it. Experiencing all of that, why would they ever consider worshipping another god? Why would they bow their knee to Baal?

Baal worship wasn't a new thing in ancient times. This powerful pagan god was symbolized as a lightning bolt, who brought rain, plentiful harvests and prosperity. He was the god of fertility and multiplication. The Israelites were very much aware of this god and those who worshipped him. They served only one God – Jehovah. But slowly Baal worship would become part of their culture.

Would God bring judgment on Israel? Or would He be merciful instead? Would they refuse the temptation to worship Baal and stay true to only one God? The Book of Judges tells us what happened. When God was going to judge Israel, He did not raise up a prophet, He gave power to a judge. With the judge in charge, Israel responded positively, backed away from Baal worship and served God alone. But when the judge died, Israel made a quick about face and turned back to Baal. God, who had given Israel a chance to serve Him alone, brought judgment on the nation.

Throughout the history of Israel, they made the choice to bow their knee to other gods. Baal was just one of the many pagan deities. In the Book of Matthew, Jesus called Satan Beelzebub, Baal of Zebub. Beelzebub, the god of Baal. Baal worship and the worship of other deities was everywhere, but it was scattered and somewhat hidden. At one point it was not tolerated by Israel at all. But just like the frog in the pan. Israel changed their mind repeatedly. Over time they moved farther away from the God of Abraham, Isaac and Jacob.

With this scriptural perspective in mind, think about what's ahead for us as believers. Take a moment and think about the next seven years. Will you experience 7 years of fat or 7 years of lean? Remember the years are not one after the other, they are side by side. Not everyone will be blessed. There will be some, side by side with the prosperous, that will be living lean. You could be fat and happy and someone you know could be lean.

Think for a moment about a few things. I believe the election of President Donald J. Trump was a sign. I want to remind you that I am not focusing on politics. This isn't about Republicans, Democrats or Independents or other governmental policies. Currently we have a president that is pro-Christianity and pro-Israel. He is standing strong with Israel and Middle East allies. Genesis 12:3 is clear. God declares.

"³I will bless those who bless you, And I will curse him who curses you;" (Genesis 12:3)

Almighty God, Maker of the Universe is making this statement. His words are to both individuals and to nations alike. If we curse Israel, God Himself will curse us. If we bless Israel, Almighty God, who changes not, will bless us.

Blessing and Cursing

In the Book of Deuteronomy, Chapter 30, verse 19 God delivers a warning to all that have ears to hear.

"¹⁹ I call heaven and earth as witnesses today against you, *that* I have set before you life and death, blessing and cursing; therefore choose life, that both you and your descendants may live." (Deuteronomy 30:19)

If President Trump is re-elected he will serve a total of eight years in office. I believe, that his election and potential re-election is connected to the 7 years of fat and the blessings God has in store for those who have "eyes to see." Just like President Truman, President Trump is playing a critical part in history, the future of Israel and prophecy.

At midnight on May 14, 1948, the provisional government proclaimed a new state of Israel. On that same day, President Truman issued a proclamation recognizing the nation of Israel. He was the first to do so. As a sovereign nation, the United States was at that time and continues to be a blessing to Israel and the Jewish people. God commanded a blessing on our nation then and He will continue to do so now. Because we have chosen to bless Israel, God has brought abundant blessings and prosperity to the United States of America.

Like President Harry S. Truman, President Trump took an unprecedented step. On December 6, 2017, speaking from the Diplomatic Room of the White House, he declared "Today we finally acknowledge the obvious that Jerusalem is Israel's capital. This is nothing more than a recognition of reality. It's also the right thing to do." He continued, taking a step that previous presidents had promised but never delivered – moving the U.S. Embassy from Tel Aviv to Jerusalem.

Prime Minister Benjamin Netanyahu during his most recent visit to the U.S. on March 5th, 2018 issued a personal invitation to President Trump to attend the opening of the U.S. embassy in May, during the nation's 70th anniversary celebration. He is expected to accept that invitation. To those of us who have eyes to see each of these steps are both historic and prophetic!

President Trump's courageous decision to declare Jerusalem as the capital of Israel and move the embassy there is something no other president, and no other nation, had been willing to do since Israel became a nation in 1948. Just as President Truman's recognition of Israel as a sovereign nation released God's blessing on the U.S., so will President Trump's biblical declaration in support of Israel and Jerusalem.

What's next for America and Israel? The answer depends on us. If the current Vice President, Mike Pence, runs for president after President Trump's tenure, I believe God's blessing and favor will continue. He is a man who also loves God and has consistently supported Israel and the Jewish people.

If we pull back, lose our resolve or let our spiritual oil run out there will be a different outcome. If we fall asleep, choose to walk in darkness and ignore God's signs, the 7 lean cows will eat the 7 fat cows and His blessing will no longer be released in our lives. I am convinced one of the reasons why President Trump was elected was because the Church "woke up," prayed and acted. We dodged a bullet when God put President Trump in office.

Not too long ago, one of the talk show hosts on the daytime television show "The View" said that Vice President Pence's comment that he hears from God were "dangerous" and an indication of "mental Illness." Two men being interviewed for judgeships some time ago were disqualified because of their "religious" beliefs. This is hard to believe, but it happened right here in America. We can't stand by and watch the erosion of Judeo-Christian values in our culture. As Christians we must stand united, pray and act on God's Word so that we can remain "One Nation under God."

The Church must repent and return to God. If we as believers refuse to live within the commandments of God. If we bow our knee to the world and its gods and don't serve God alone. We will be facing the judgment the Israelites endured in the Book of Judges.

I pray and believe in my heart, that God is extending His grace for the next seven years. But while we have time, we need to repent and return to God. If we don't, America and the world will continue to change and move away from God and toward destruction.

We cannot stand by while God is removed from our schools and erased from our government. We need to stand up for our God-given rights and Word-based values. We have a choice. We can return to God, where we are one nation under God, not Allah or Krishna. Our God is Jehovah, the God of Abraham, Isaac and Jacob.

As believers and children of God we need to stand against evil. We need to make sure we don't slide into the worship of other gods. Remember that Baal slowly became part of Israel's culture. It didn't happen overnight. People in America are saying things like "Jehovah's good, but there are other gods. He's not the only God." "There are many ways to God." I don't believe that. Do you?

Recently I heard a Catholic priest respond to this type of thinking by saying "Why don't we just call God Allah? Because God's name is not Allah. God's name is Jehovah. We will have no other gods before Him." Some might call this narrowmindedness, but it's not. It is truth and we need to be declaring it. We can't be like the Israelites who traded the faithfulness of God Almighty for the impotence of the pagan god Baal.

God had brought them out of Egypt. He had provided for them in the wilderness and given them the land He promised them. But they chose not to serve Him. They chose Baal. We can't do that. We must make the right choice – God alone. He has given us a land of promise where we can worship and serve Him. Just like that courageous Catholic priest, we must speak up and stand up for what we believe. We need to be the frog that jumps out of the pan.

Baal worship started when the Israelites embraced other gods for economic profits. They exchanged the truth of God for a lie and embraced false teaching.

Their disobedience didn't stop there. They allowed sexual immortality, saying "Since we have gotten rid of 'one God' let's forget what He says." They accepted not only the worship of Baal in the temples, but they brought in prostitutes. They encouraged sexual immorality.

Step by step, they got farther away from God. They agreed with the immoral. "If sexual relationships don't matter and there are more choices then just men with women, then let's let people do what they want." They endorsed homosexuality.

Now the frog isn't feeling the pain, but the heat is rising. The water is almost a full boil. Next, they did the unthinkable. They offered their children to Baal. They placed their sons and daughters on the fires of his altar. For generations the unborn have been sacrificed through abortion.

The Bible says that in the last days there will be a "great falling away." That doesn't mean the doors of the church will close, just that the truth of God's Word won't be taught anymore. Places of worship will still exist, but their parishioners will have thrown God out and brought Baal in.

The Israelites chose Baal. We have stood by and watched others systematically remove God from every area of life. He is no longer a part of government. His Word is no longer allowed to be taught to children in schools. The "10 Commandments" and God have been erased from the courts and justice system.

I went to a high school football game recently. They started the game with a moment of silence. I can remember when I played football. We started the game with prayer. We pledged allegiance to the flag. Now they kneel in protest.

In America, we have gone from tolerance to acceptance to endorsement. But it's not too late. We can still be the frog that jumps from the pan. The water is heating up, but we can still reverse the present direction and return to God. It's not too late for America or any place in the world.

We need to wake up and call on the God of Abraham, Isaac and Jacob and repent and return to Him. I believe God is going to bring great revival throughout the earth. When Jesus returns we are going to be a glorious Bride without spot, blemish or wrinkle. We are going to occupy until He comes. We are going to bring in a mighty harvest of souls for the Kingdom of God.

I am not tolerant. I am the opposite. I will not allow Beelzebub to destroy our country, families and churches. God used Elijah to defeat Baal and his false prophets, "Maybe your god can't hear you" Elijah said. He cried out to the great "I AM." God heard his prayer and answered with a lightning bolt of fire that destroyed all the prophets of Baal.

God was declaring to the world of that day, "Baal is not the one who will bring provision for you, I am Jehovah Jireh. I am your provider." God destroyed the altars of Baal. He obliterated his prophets. We must be like Elijah and stand against the evil around us. We do not battle with flesh and blood but against principalities, powers and rulers of darkness in high places. We have a God who hears us and is all powerful.

I declare to you, and pray that you agree with me, that Beelzebub, the god of this world is already defeated. We will put God back on the throne in America. We will serve only one God, the God of Abraham, Isaac and Jacob. We will, once again, become "One Nation under God" and fulfill our prophetic purpose and destiny.

ABOUT THE AUTHOR

Larry Huch and his wife Tiz are founders and senior pastors of New Beginnings Church in Bedford, Texas. Their congregation extends via live streamed services to their satellite church in Portland, Oregon and to partners and friends around the world.

Pastor Huch is a recognized authority and writer on the Jewish roots of the Christian faith including "The Torah Blessing" "Unveiling Ancient Biblical Secrets" "The 4 Blood Moons – The Future Begins Now!" "The Jubilee Blessing" and this new book "Bible Prophecy – Signs of the Times."

He has also written the timeless classics, "Free At Last" "7 Places Jesus Shed His Blood" and "10 Curses That Block the Blessing." He and Tiz co-authored the book "Releasing Family Blessings."

Larry Huch Ministries is dedicated, without question, to standing with Israel and the Jewish people and building bridges of peace, friendship and unity between Christians and Jews. Their commitment to making a difference and practicing the Jewish concept of "tikkun olam" - repairing a broken world has resulted in many projects and outreaches that have positively impacted thousands upon thousands of lives in Israel and around the world.

Larry Huch Ministries
PO Box 610890
Dallas, TX 75261
1-800-978-8546
www.larryhuchministries.com